NFL★TODAY

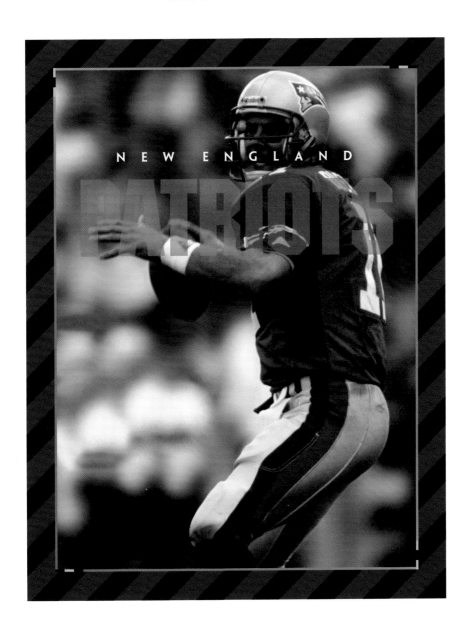

NEW ENGLAND PATRIOTS

STEVE POTTS

CREATIVE ✿ EDUCATION

Published by Creative Education
123 South Broad Street, Mankato, Minnesota 56001
Creative Education is an imprint of The Creative Company

Designed by Rita Marshall
Cover illustration by Rob Day

Photos by: Allsport Photography, Associated Press, Bettmann Archive, Duomo,
Focus on Sports, Fotosport, FPG International, and SportsChrome.

Library of Congress Cataloging-in-Publication Data

Potts, Steve, 1956-
New England Patriots / by Steve Potts.
p. cm. — (NFL Today)
Summary: Traces the history of the team from its beginnings through 1996.
ISBN 0-88682-801-5

1. New England Patriots (Football team)—History—Juvenile literature.
[1. New England Patriots (Football team) 2. Football—History.]
I. Title. II. Series.

GV956.N36P68   1996   96-15241
796.332'64'0974461—dc20

123456

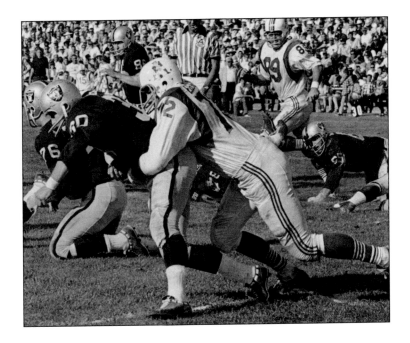

Many of the early American colonists who left England for the New World wound up settling in what is now the northeastern United States. These settlers called their new land New England after their former home. Even today, the northeastern United States is known as New England, a region that includes Massachusetts, New Hampshire, Connecticut, Rhode Island, Vermont and Maine.

The largest city in New England is Boston, Massachusetts. Since its founding in the 1600s, Boston has been the center of political and economic life in New England. Boston was also the scene for much of the activity that led to the Revolutionary

Linebacker Nick Buoniconti.

1 9 6 1

Receiver Gino Cappelletti did double duty as the Patriots' kicker, scoring 60 points.

War. In 1773, a group of colonists, upset at what they considered to be an unfair tax on their favorite drink—tea—climbed aboard a British ship anchored in Boston Harbor and threw 342 containers filled with tea into the water. This incident is remembered today as the Boston Tea Party. In 1775, Paul Revere made his famous ride from Lexington to Concord—two towns on the outskirts of Boston—to warn colonists that British troops were marching to Concord to destroy the colonists' munitions supply.

Those colonists who wanted independence from British rule were called patriots. The Boston area was home to many patriots. Today, Boston is still home to Patriots, but these Patriots aren't fighting the British. They are struggling to make it to the top of the National Football League. The New England Patriots, the team that took their name from American history, are strong fighters like the patriots of long ago.

When the team was first formed in 1960, it was known as the Boston Patriots. The Patriots, or Pats for short, joined seven other teams as original members of the American Football League. Boston had some success in the AFL's first years. Stars like quarterback Babe Parilli, receiver Gino Cappelletti and linebacker Nick Buoniconti led the team to many of their early victories. In 1963, the Patriots tied the Buffalo Bills for first place in their division, then crushed the Bills 26-8 in the playoffs. But when Boston met San Diego to play for the AFL title, the Chargers trounced the Patriots 51-10. It would be a long 22 years before the Patriots again found themselves in a league championship game.

Today Andre Tippett continues the Patriots' great linebacker tradition (page 7).

1 9 7 1

*Jim Plunkett, stand-
out quarterback
from Stanford, was
the Patriots' number
one draft pick.*

The Patriots finished second in their division in 1964, but then struggled to a 4-8-2 record in 1965, the worst record in their six-year existence. Luckily, the 1965 season also saw the arrival of a gifted player who could help the ailing Patriots: Syracuse University running back Jim Nance. Such NFL and AFL star running backs as Jim Brown, Ernie Davis, Floyd Little and Larry Csonka were also Syracuse graduates, so Nance was part of a long tradition of winners.

Nance came to the Patriots as a ninth-round draft pick. During his college career, he never reached what he felt was his full potential. He played backup to the great Floyd Little, but Nance felt he was better than just a backup player. His anger led him to eat. And eat. And eat. By the time he reported to the Patriots training camp in the summer of 1965, Patriots coaches understood why "Big Bo" was the nickname given to their new fullback. Nance weighed in at 260 pounds, a higher weight than that of most of the Patriots linemen. Despite his weight, Nance was strong and fast. Coach Mike Holovak, seeing Nance's speed, told the rookie that he had the potential to make it as a running back. But Nance had trouble adjusting to the pro level and played poorly. Holovak gave Nance a choice: "You block pretty well. How would you like to be switched to guard? If you don't get your weight down in a hurry, next week you start working out with the linemen."

Nance, no stranger to hard work, set out to lose weight. He didn't want to play guard. Nance dropped 14 pounds in a week and won the position as starting fullback. A year later, he came to the 1966 training camp weighing a trim 235 pounds and eager to play. His hard work paid off. Nance pushed hard enough to set an AFL record of 1,458 rushing yards. The Patriots were on their way back to the top and Nance was feared as one of the league's strongest backs.

Nance believed in the power of the mind over the body and used his determination to prepare for games. He ate his last pregame meal sixteen hours before the kickoff. "Hunger makes me mad," he said, and by kickoff his stomach was growling and his anger was ready to spill over onto the football field.

1 9 7 1

In his rookie season, quarterback Jim Plunkett threw for 2,158 yards and 19 touchdowns.

Nance also made a practice of running over, not around, people. "I've been noticing that when a guy hits me head-on, he's not quite so quick to hit me the next time," Nance mused. "So I keep running at him, and pretty soon he wants to turn his shoulder. Then I know I've got him. When a man turns his shoulder on me, I'm going to get past him before he turns back."

Even Nance couldn't save his team from a losing season in 1967, however, when the Patriots turned in a dismal 3-10-1 showing that earned them a last place finish. And that wasn't the worst. They became notorious for their poor fan attendance, which was so low that the team hadn't even invested in building a permanent home field. By the time the AFL and NFL merged in 1970, the Patriots had called five different fields home in their first ten years. They finally settled upon Schaefer Stadium in Foxboro, Massachusetts in 1971. In honor of the team's new location on the outskirts of Boston, team owner Billy Sullivan changed its name to the New England Patriots.

HANNAH HANDLES THEM ON THE LINE

Building a winner takes time, but all the Patriots' hard work paid off. Slowly but surely, they were gathering players

Drew Bledsoe emerged as the Patriots' quarterback of the 1990s (pages 10-11).

Rookie quarterback Steve Grogan joined the Patriots for what would be a 16-year career.

who would add power to their team. The first of these additions was John Hannah, a 6-foot-2 offensive lineman. At 265 pounds, Hannah was amazingly strong, but he also had remarkable athletic talents for a man his size. Hannah, at his best, was one of the NFL's all-time great offensive linemen. "For all his size and explosiveness and straight-ahead speed," New England general manager Bucko Kilroy reflected, "John has something none of the others ever had. And that's phenomenal—repeat, phenomenal—lateral agility and balance, the same as defensive backs have. You'll watch his man stunt around the opposite end, and John will just stay with him. He'll slide along like a toe dancer, on tippy-toe. And that's a 270-pound man doing that, a guy capable of positively annihilating an opponent."

A mark of true talent is when other players praise your abilities, and Hannah certainly had his fans. Jim Parker, Pro Football Hall of Famer and among the best offensive linemen ever to play in the NFL, praised Hannah as "the only one out there who can do it all—every aspect. I pray he doesn't get hurt, but the way he plays football, I don't think he will, because he gives it everything he has. If you want me to rate myself compared to him, I'll say that I sure would have enjoyed playing alongside him."

Hannah had a few problems adjusting to pro football at first, but that soon changed. He worked hard on the field and spent hours watching game films. Once he became a perennial All-Pro, opponents began looking for ways to make Hannah look bad. But the Patriots' star lineman relished the challenge. "One thing I found out," Hannah said, "was that the guy you'd see on film wasn't always the same player you'd meet on the field.

If they thought you were one of the best, they'd get all fired up and play over their heads." And Hannah wasn't one to let them get away with mistakes.

GROGAN GETS A CHANCE AND RUNS WITH IT

1 9 7 6

Wide receiver Darryl Stingley caught 17 passes and averaged 22 yards per catch.

Although Hannah's job was to protect the Patriots quarterback, the team had a hard time finding a quality signal caller. Stanford University star quarterback Jim Plunkett was drafted in 1971 to fill this gap, but Plunkett had trouble fitting in with the Patriots. After a 3-11 finish in 1975, the Patriots sent Plunkett to the San Francisco 49ers and turned to backup quarterback Steve Grogan. Grogan was experienced and had the advantage of knowing the Patriots' system.

The gamble paid off. Grogan's passing and running turned the Patriots around and led them to an 11-3 record in 1976. With his ability to scramble for yardage, Grogan threatened opponents with both his strong arm and his speed. "I've already believed in trying to take advantage of the abilities your players have," Patriots coach Chuck Fairbanks said, "and Steve is a threat as a runner."

Grogan was also the driving force behind the Patriots. "He's our leader, our motivator," Hannah said. "When we need big plays, he comes up with them. There's only a few quarterbacks who will do what Steve does now. He holds that ball. He'll sit there, hold it, he'll get that lick, and then throw. It makes you want to give up a little bit of your life for him."

Grogan's biggest challenge was adjusting to his new-found fame. From rural Kansas, Grogan had trouble feeling at home in big cities. "We don't have anything like Boston in Kansas,"

1 9 7 7

Tight end Russ Francis averaged 14 yards per catch and excelled at blocking.

the shy Grogan mused. "I'm not used to going out shopping or to the movies and always being recognized. How do I handle it? I handle it by staying home."

The shy Kansan may have tried to dodge his fame, but New England fans were thrilled with their new team leader. The Patriots reached the playoffs in 1976 and almost pulled off a huge upset. In their first playoff game, they met the Raiders in Oakland. The Raiders expected to roll over New England, but were shocked when the Patriots took a 21-10 lead early in the game's second half. Raiders quarterback Kenny Stabler brought his team back in a last quarter rally that clinched a 24-21 victory and brought an end to one of football's most thrilling games. The Raiders blitzed through the rest of their playoff games to win the Super Bowl, but much of the attention in 1976 was on the Patriots. The experts were convinced that New England was the team of the future in the AFC.

The Patriots had a bright collection of young stars to go along with Grogan and Hannah. Offensive leaders included fullback Sam Cunningham, wide receiver Darryl Stingley, tackle Leon Gray and tight end Russ Francis. Cunningham went all out for every yard, often making the difference at the goal line with his powerful running and agility. Stingley had the ability to snatch passes from the air and weave his way to the end zone. Gray teamed up with Hannah to make a fearsome duo. Francis, towering above his teammates at 6-foot-6 and a hefty 240 pounds, made miraculous catches, leading many observers to consider him the finest tight end in the NFL.

The Patriots defense was anchored by linemen Julius Adams and Ray Hamilton, while linebackers Steve Nelson and Rod Shoate were on top of opponents everywhere along the line. Two bright future prospects, cornerback Mike Haynes and safety Tim Fox, joined the roster in 1976.

Hart Lee Dykes hoped to surpass Morgan's team records.   15

1 9 7 8

Cornerback Tim Fox was a stalwart pass defender in the Patriots' secondary.

The 1977 college draft added two more stars to the Patriots' team-building effort. University of Texas running back Raymond Clayborn came to New England as a cornerback, where he and Mike Haynes became a prized pair of one-on-one pass defenders. Stanley Morgan, a sprinter from the University of Tennessee, joined Darryl Stingley to produce a speedy set of wide receivers.

But hopes of a 1977 Super Bowl season ended with a pre-season contract dispute between Hannah and Gray and team management. Both players refused to practice or play until they got better contracts and more money. Hannah eventually came to terms with the Patriots and played, but Gray was traded to New Orleans. The fine Hannah-Gray combination was broken up. The team faltered, losing four games early in the 1977 season. Although they recovered and ended the season at a respectable 9-5, they failed to make the playoffs.

Even though they had a disappointing 1977 season, sports commentators were convinced the Patriots would make it back to the playoffs in 1978. But a pre-season game against the Oakland Raiders proved tragic for the team. Steve Grogan wafted a pass to Darryl Stingley. Stingley jumped to catch the high pass and collided in midair with Oakland defenseman Jack Tatum. Stingley hit the turf hard and didn't get up. Patriots doctors came onto the field, tested his reflexes and, fearing the worst, put the injured receiver on a stretcher and took him to the hospital. Doctors found that Stingley's neck was broken and that he was paralyzed from his shoulders down. Stingley was now a quadriplegic and his career had come to an abrupt end.

Stingley's accident pushed the team to play their best to lift

Patriots cornerback Mike Haynes excelled at grabbing interceptions.   17

the spirits of their injured teammate. This momentum brought them the AFC Eastern Division title in 1978, but they lost their first playoff game to the Houston Oilers 31-14. Coach Chuck Fairbanks, frustrated by his inability to reach the Super Bowl, left pro football to coach at the University of Colorado. He left a winning team, but unfortunately his successor Ron Erhardt wasn't able to turn the frustrated Patriots into champions during his three years as coach.

New England owner Billy Sullivan fired Erhardt and brought in Ron Meyer, who immediately set out to mold a winning club. He traded veterans Russ Francis, Rod Shoate and Tim Fox in exchange for future draft choices. These draft choices were used to bring star defensemen Kenneth Sims and Andre Tippett to New England. In 1983, Meyer used another draft choice to add quarterback Tony Eason to the team. But Meyer's changes did

not produce an immediate winner, so he was fired in 1984.

New coach Raymond Berry brought long years of football experience to New England. Berry was an All-Pro receiver with the Baltimore Colts and had been an assistant coach with New England, where he helped turn Darryl Stingley and Stanley Morgan into stars. In 1985, Berry's experience paid off. Steve Grogan, who battled Tony Eason to retain his quarterback job and endured angry Patriots fans who booed him on the field, came back from a string of down years to record a stellar season in 1985. "I don't care for being booed," Grogan said. "I want to prove myself to the people here."

Grogan led a comeback win over Miami in the regular season's final week that clinched a playoff spot for the Patriots. Coach Berry, eager to emphasize a running game in the playoffs, brought in Eason to quarterback the team. Eason rarely passed, but running backs Craig James and Tony Collins moved the ball well enough that New England dominated the New York Jets, Los Angeles Raiders and Miami Dolphins in the playoffs. After a decade of proving themselves, the Patriots finally reached the Super Bowl. Unfortunately they were up against the Chicago Bears, a team with a magnificent 15-1 regular-season record. Chicago rolled over the Patriots by a 46-10 margin. Although it was a disappointing loss, the Patriots had nothing to be ashamed of. They had climbed to the top and proved that dedication could produce a winning team.

1 9 8 4

Head coach Raymond Berry took over in mid-season and immediately provided steady leadership.

STANLEY STEAMS BACK TO THE TOP

As the Patriots approached the 1986 season, their prospects seemed improved when Stanley "Steamer" Morgan, nicknamed "Steamer" because of his impressive speed,

Craig James was a fearsome rusher in the 1980s.

returned healthy to training camp. Morgan had made two trips to the Pro Bowl in the early 1980s, but coach Ron Meyer rarely allowed Morgan much playing time. Morgan, angry at the situation, developed a bad attitude. "I got lazy," he said, "and got into some bad habits." He began dropping crucial passes and, by 1986, even some teammates thought that Morgan, now more than thirty years old, had reached the end of his career.

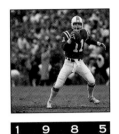

Quarterback Tony Eason passed for over 2,100 yards and eleven touchdowns.

But Morgan wasn't finished yet. When Coach Berry took over, he knew from his days as a Patriots assistant coach that Morgan had great potential. Morgan regained his confidence and his health and turned in an amazing season. "I was excited about playing football again," Morgan declared, and his excitement showed. He set a team record with 84 pass receptions, including 10 touchdown receptions. In nine games he received for at least 100 yards.

Morgan's last great clutch grab in the 1986 season reminded skeptics of why the 10-year veteran was so highly valued. With 44 seconds left to play, New England and Miami were tied. New England's ball sat on the Miami 30-yard line. This was a make-or-break play. A win would get New England into the playoffs. As they huddled, Grogan gazed around at the small group of determined men, then turned to Morgan and asked if he could get open. "Sure," Morgan said softly. "No problem."

As they turned from the huddle and went down for the play, Grogan took the ball, faded back, looked for Morgan, then lobbed a long pass up the right sideline into Morgan's waiting hands— in the end zone. That touchdown won the game for the Patriots and clinched a playoff berth. In what turned out to be their last playoff game under Berry, the Patriots lost in a close game to the Denver Broncos, 22-17.

Over the next two seasons, the Patriots' fortunes declined.

24   *Left to right: John Stephens, Stanley Morgan, Andre Tippett, Tony Collins.*

But their hopes were raised again for the 1989 season. The New England defense contained plenty of raw talent. Andre Tippett kept his linebacker skills honed by practicing the martial arts. He was multitalented: he rushed passers, ran down ball carriers and pushed downfield to block passes. He and cornerback Ronnie Lippett frustrated their opponents by hanging close to them.

On the offensive side, there was reason for hope as well. John Stephens, a rookie in 1988, had proved to be a pleasant surprise. Not highly rated as he came out of college, he ran 1,168 yards to finish second in the AFC in rushing. He also played in the Pro Bowl as a rookie.

But the bad luck that dogged the Patriots returned in 1989. Tippett was hurt in the last pre-season game and missed the regular season. The Patriots' defense had holes torn in it by his absence. At age 36, Steve Grogan needed a backup, but the Patriots had no other effective quarterback. Stephens played most of the season with injuries. With all these problems, New England's 5-11 record was no surprise. The Patriots fired Raymond Berry and decided upon a new coach to rebuild their ailing team.

Veteran receiver Stanley Morgan snared 28 passes and averaged 17.4 yards per catch.

AIMING FOR THE HEIGHTS IN THE 1990s

Rod Rust, who was defensive coordinator for New England's Super Bowl team, was selected to replace Berry. Rust came to a team that was much healthier. In 1990, Tippett returned to the regular lineup. John Stephens, too, was back at full strength, and determined Steve Grogan beat out the young quarterbacks who were brought in to replace him. As it turned

Rookie Curtis Martin displayed his running skills in 1995 (pages 26-27).

1 9 9 6

Head coach Bill Parcells provides the Patriots with proven NFL leadership skills.

out, however, 1990 proved to be one of the Patriots' worst seasons. Finishing with a 1-15 record, the Patriots had gone from embarrassing to horrible. Rust was dismissed and a new head coach, Dick MacPherson, came on board in 1991. But his tenure did not lead to much improvement. New England finished 1991 with a 6-10 record and dropped to 2-14 in 1992.

Bill Parcells—who had led the New York Giants to two Super Bowl victories—took over as head coach in 1993. At that point, the Patriots had suffered through four losing seasons in a row. Fans missed the familiar faces from the team's glory days in the 1980s. Stanley Morgan was the first to go in 1989, and Steve Grogan left a year later. Ronnie Lippett and Garin Veris departed in 1991, Andre Tippett in 1993 and the popular John Stephens in 1992.

Parcells came to New England determined to reverse their tailspin and mold another winning team. Eight seasons with the Giants had taught Parcells how to create winners. He demonstrated his talents by using the Patriots' No. 1 pick in the 1993 NFL Draft to snare star quarterback Drew Bledsoe out of Washington State. Bledsoe, a rambunctious 21-year-old when he was drafted, soon began to show the determination and coolness under pressure that pointed toward a long and rewarding career in pro football.

Bledsoe and Parcells developed a unique relationship built on their mutual respect for each other. This didn't mean that the demanding coach always agreed with his young star. "He's learned some things," Parcell admitted, "but not all of the things he does are good." Bledsoe, famed for his relaxed, easygoing nature, praised his coach as a "smart guy," but said that Parcells "turns the pressure up in practice when we're not winning. That's the hard part. You almost never see me fired up and ticked off. I still look at this as fun."

Brent Williams was a stalwart defender in the 1990s.

Running back Curtis Martin, destined to become a star.

Quarterback Drew Bledsoe demonstrated his star ability in the 1990s.   31

Number one draft pick Terry Glenn is a valuable addition to the Patriots' wide receiving corps.

And fun it was for such a successful young player. In 1994, his second NFL season, Bledsoe attempted a record 691 passes and completed 400, only four short of Warren Moon's all-time NFL completion record. He passed for an amazing 4,555 yards in that season, a feat matched by few quarterbacks. It landed him in the Pro Bowl as the youngest quarterback ever to play in that game. Bledsoe's heroics benefited the team as well. The Patriots finished 10-6 in 1994 and returned to the play-offs at last.

With Bledsoe and other young standouts like rookie running back Curtis Martin, nicknamed "Moses" and the "Golden Child" by his teammates, the Patriots seemed headed in the right direction. Although the Patriots finished their 1995 season with a disappointing 6-10 record, New England's avid football fans continue to support the Patriots. Those fans can look to the future with justified optimism. A return to the Super Bowl may be just around the corner.